Christmas Songs for Ukulele

Arranged by Barrett Tagliarino

ISBN 978-0-634-06088-5

HAL•LEONARD®
CORPORATION

7777 W. BLUEMOUND RD. P.O. BOX 13819 MILWAUKEE, WI 53213

Visit Hal Leonard Online at
www.halleonard.com

Blue Christmas

Words and Music by Billy Hayes and Jay Johnson

First note

Moderate shuffle

I'll have a blue Christ-mas with-out you. _____

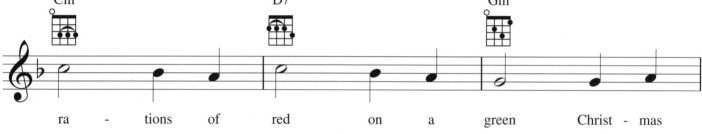

_____ I'll be so blue think-ing a-bout you. _____ Dec-o-

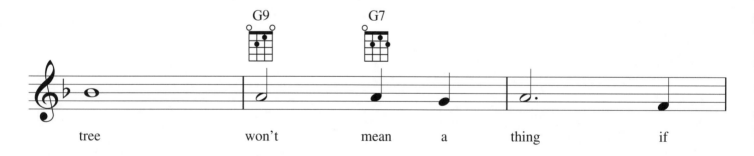

ra - tions of red on a green Christ-mas

tree won't mean a thing if

you're not here with me. _____ I'll have a

blue   Christ - mas,   that's   cer - tain _____

____   and   when   that   blue   heart - ache   starts

hurt - in', _____   you'll   be

do - in'   all   right,   with   your

Christ - mas   of   white,   but   I'll   have   a

blue,   blue   Christ - mas. _____

The Christmas Song
(Chestnuts Roasting on an Open Fire)

Music and Lyric by Mel Torme and Robert Wells

night.   They know that   San - ta's on his   way;   he's load-ed

lots of toys and good-ies on his sleigh.   And ev-'ry moth-er's child ___ is gon-na

spy _____ to see if rein-deer ___ real-ly know how to   fly.   And

so, I'm of-fer-ing this sim-ple phrase   to kids from one to nine-ty-

two.   Al-tho' it's been said man-y   times man-y ways, "Mer-ry

Christ - mas   to   you."

Christmas Time Is Here

from A CHARLIE BROWN CHRISTMAS

Words by Lee Mendelson
Music by Vince Guaraldi

First note

Slowly

Christ - mas time is here,
Snow - flakes in the air,

hap - pi - ness and cheer.
car - ols ev - 'ry - where.
Fun for all that
Old - en times and

chil - dren call their fa - v'rite time of year.
an - cient rhymes of love and dreams to share.

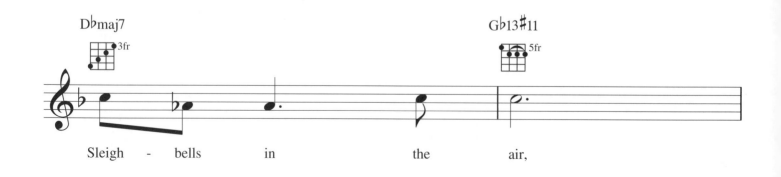

Sleigh - bells in the air,

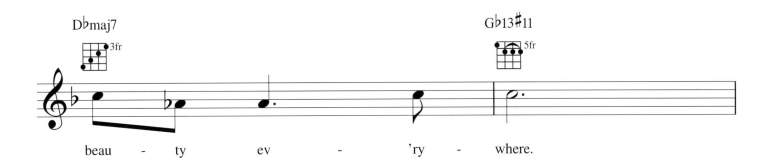

beau - ty ev - 'ry - where.

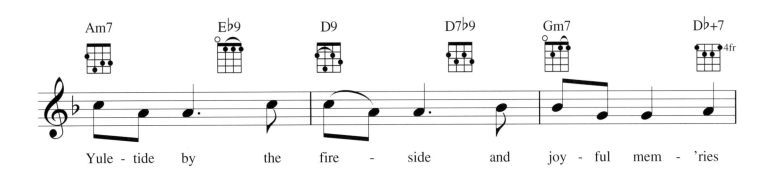

Yule - tide by the fire - side and joy - ful mem - 'ries

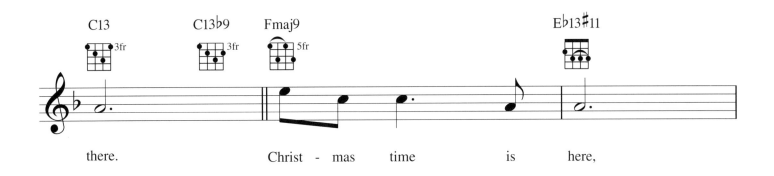

there. Christ - mas time is here,

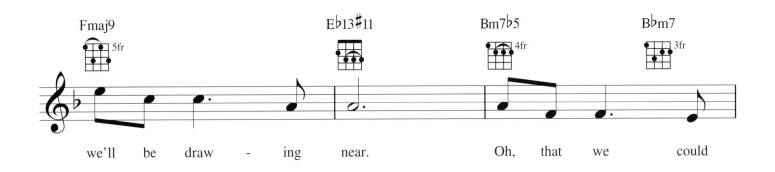

we'll be draw - ing near. Oh, that we could

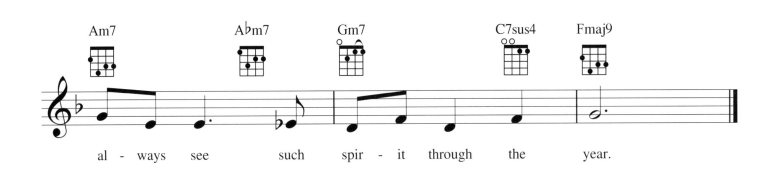

al - ways see such spir - it through the year.

Do You Hear What I Hear

Words and Music by Noel Regney and Gloria Shayne

lit - tle lamb   to the shep - herd boy,   "Do you hear what I   hear?
king   to the peo - ple ev - 'ry - where,   "Lis - ten to what I   say!

Ring - ing thru the sky shep - herd boy.
Pray for peace, people ev - 'ry - where.

Do you hear what I   hear?"   A song,   a song,
Lis - ten to what I   say!"   The Child,   the Child,

high a - bove the tree, with a   voice   as   big   as the sea,   with a
sleep - ing in the night, He will bring   us   good - ness and light,   He will

1.
voice   as   big   as the sea.   3. Said the

2.
bring   us   good - ness   and   light.

11

Feliz Navidad

Music and Lyrics by José Feliciano

I want to wish you a Mer - ry Christ - mas from the

bot - tom of my heart.

I want to wish you a Mer - ry Christ - mas,

with mis - tle - toe and lots of cheer.

With lots of laugh - ter through - out the years from the

bot - tom of my heart.

Frosty the Snow Man

Words and Music by Steve Nelson and Jack Rollins

C   Dm   G7   C   G

mag - ic   in   that   old   silk   hat   they   found.   For   when   they   placed   it
streets   of   town   right   to   the   traf - fic   cop.   And   he   on - ly   paused   a

G#°7   Am   D7   G7   G+7   C

on   his   head   he   be - gan   to   dance   a - round.   Oh,   Fros - ty   the
mo - ment   when __   he   heard   him   hol - ler   "stop!"   For   Fros - ty   the

C7   F   F#°7   C   F   F#°7

Snow   Man   was   a - live   as   he   could   be,   and   the   chil - dren   say   he   could
Snow   Man   had   to   hur - ry   on   his   way,   but   he   waved   good - bye   say - in',

C   A7   Dm   G7   C

laugh   and   play   just   the   same   as   you   and   me.
"Don't   you   cry,   I'll   be   back   a - gain   some   day."

C   G°7   G

Thump - et - y   thump   thump,   thump - et - y   thump   thump,   look   at   Fros - ty   go.

G7   C

Thump - et - y   thump   thump,   thump - et - y   thump   thump,   o - ver   the   hills   of   snow.

Here Comes Santa Claus
(Right Down Santa Claus Lane)

Words and Music by Gene Autry and Oakley Haldeman

First note

Moderately bright

Here comes San - ta Claus! Here comes San - ta Claus! Right down San - ta Claus
Here comes San - ta Claus! Here comes San - ta Claus! Right down San - ta Claus

Lane!   Vix - en and Blitz - en and all his rein - deer are
Lane!   He does - n't care if you're rich or poor for he

pull - ing on the rein.   Bells are ring - ing,
loves you just the same.   San - ta knows that

chil - dren sing - ing, all is mer - ry and bright.
we're God's chil - dren; that makes ev - 'ry - thing right.

Hang your stock - ings and say your pray'rs, 'cause San - ta Claus comes to -
Fill your hearts with a Christ - mas cheer, 'cause San - ta Claus comes to -

night.
night.

Here comes San - ta Claus! Here comes San - ta Claus!
Here comes San - ta Claus! Here comes San - ta Claus!

Right down San - ta Claus Lane! He's got a bag that is
Right down San - ta Claus Lane! He'll come a - round when the

filled with toys for the boys and girls a - gain.
chimes ring out, then it's Christ - mas morn a - gain.

Hear those sleigh - bells jin - gle jan - gle, what a beau - ti - ful
Peace on earth will come to all if we just fol - low the

sight. Jump in bed, cov - er up your head, 'cause
light. Let's give thanks to the Lord a - bove, 'cause

San - ta Claus comes to - night.
San - ta Claus comes to - night.

A Holly Jolly Christmas

Music and Lyrics by Johnny Marks

First note

Moderately bright

Have a Hol-ly Jol-ly Christ-mas, it's the best time of the

year. I don't know if there'll be snow but

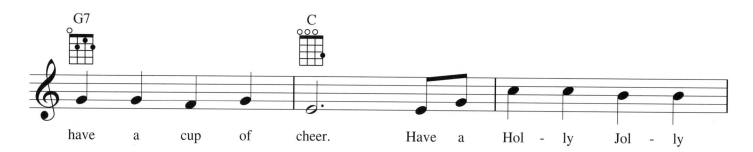

have a cup of cheer. Have a Hol-ly Jol-ly

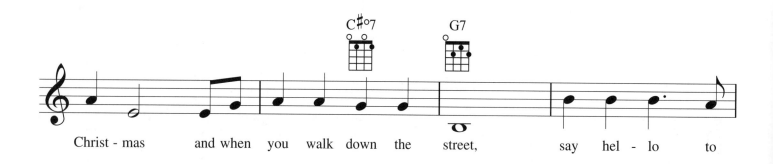

Christ-mas and when you walk down the street, say hel-lo to

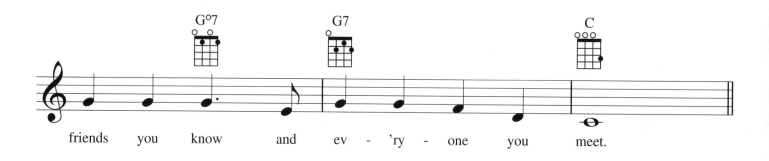

friends you know and ev-'ry-one you meet.

I Saw Mommy Kissing Santa Claus

Words and Music by Tommie Connor

First note

Moderately slow

I saw Mom - my kiss - ing San - ta

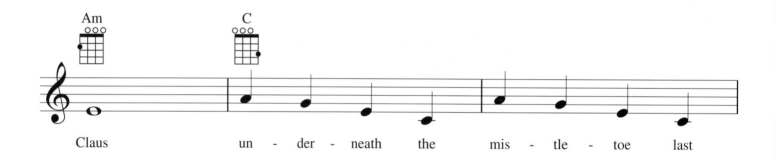

Claus un - der - neath the mis - tle - toe last

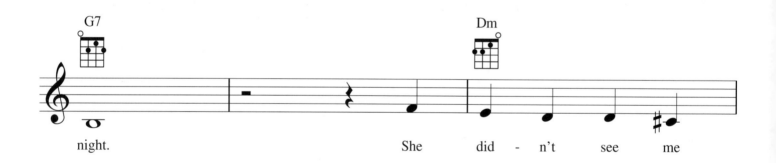

night. She did - n't see me

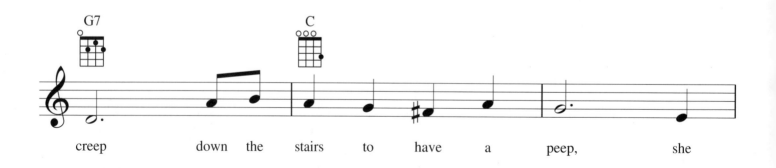

creep down the stairs to have a peep, she

thought that I was tucked up in my bed-room fast a-sleep. Then

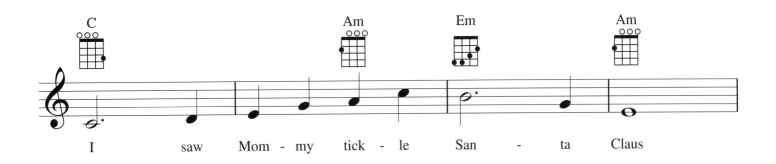

I saw Mom-my tick-le San - ta Claus

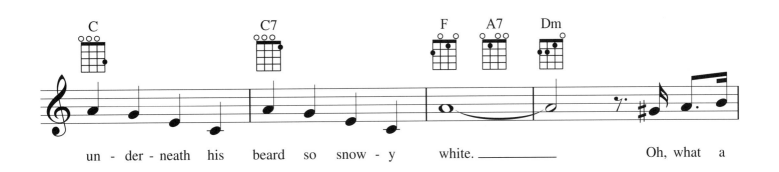

un - der-neath his beard so snow - y white. _____ Oh, what a

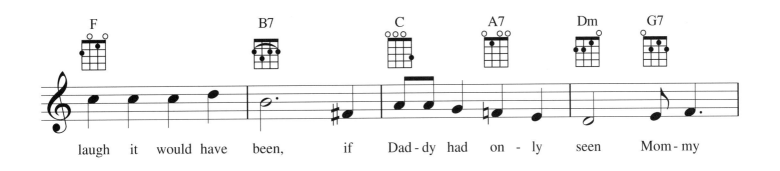

laugh it would have been, if Dad-dy had on - ly seen Mom-my

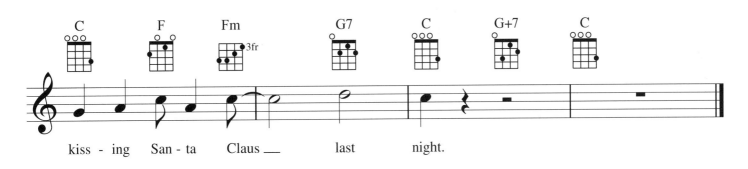

kiss - ing San - ta Claus __ last night.

I'll Be Home for Christmas

Words and Music by Kim Gannon and Walter Kent

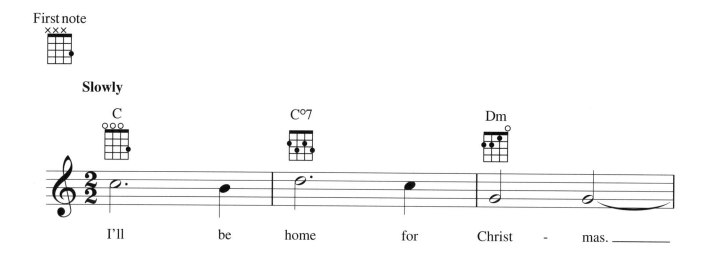

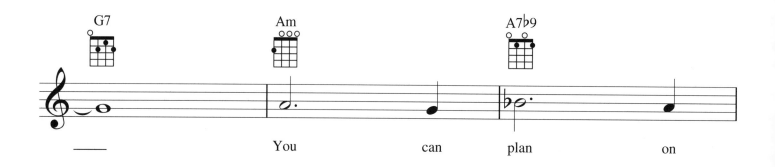

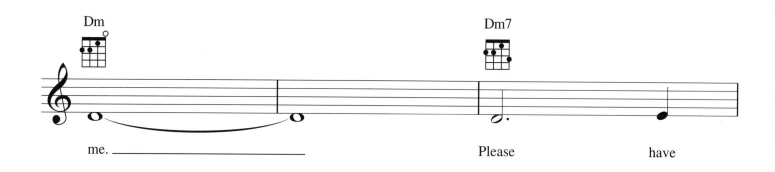

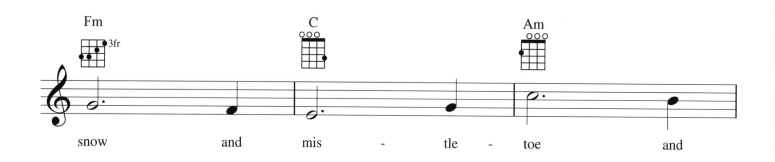

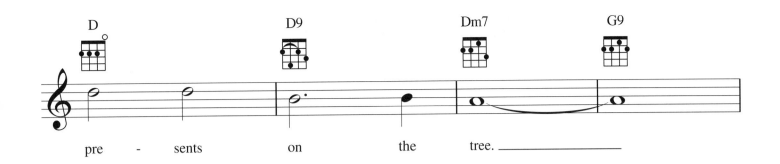

pre - sents on the tree. _____

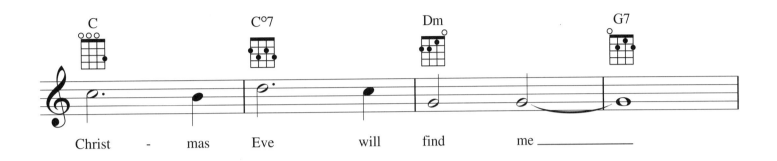

Christ - mas Eve will find me _____

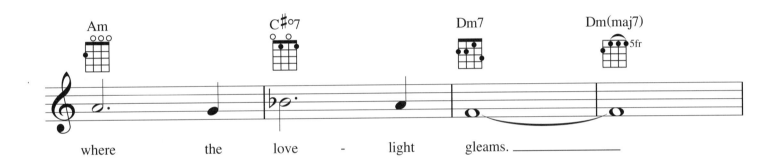

where the love - light gleams. _____

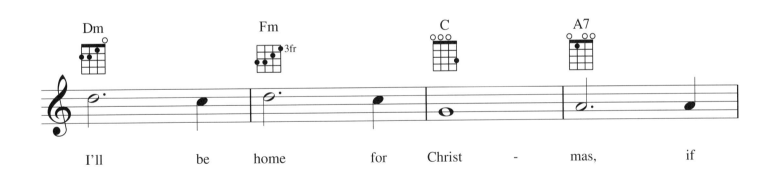

I'll be home for Christ - mas, if

on - ly in my dreams.

Jingle-Bell Rock

Words and Music by Joe Beal and Jim Boothe

Let It Snow! Let It Snow! Let It Snow!

Words by Sammy Cahn
Music by Jule Styne

snow! Let it snow! Let it snow! When we fin-al-ly kiss good-

night, how I'll hate go-ing out in the storm! But if

you'll real-ly hold me tight, all the way home I'll be

warm. The fi-re is slow-ly dy-ing, and my

dear we're still good-bye-ing. But as long as you love me

so, let it snow! Let it snow! Let it snow!

Mele Kalikimaka

Words and Music by Alex Anderson

First note

Brightly

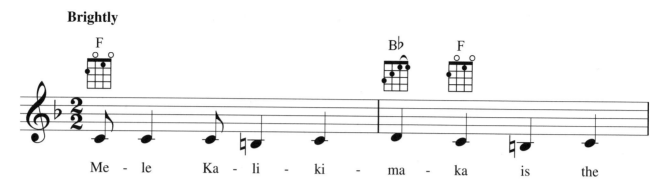

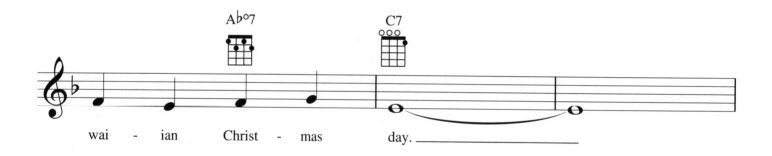

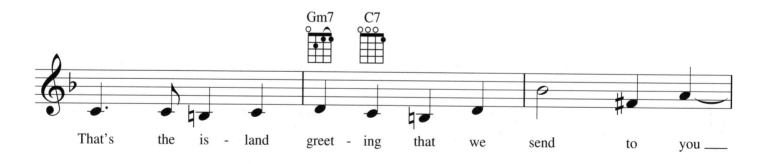

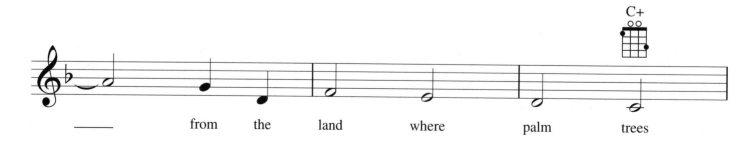

Merry Christmas, Darling

Words and Music by Richard Carpenter and Frank Pooler

Intro first note   Melody first note

Rubato

Greet-ing cards have all been sent, the Christ-mas rush is through.

But I still have one wish to make, a spe-cial one for you.

Mer-ry Christ-mas, dar-ling. We're a-part, that's true, but

I can dream and in my dreams, I'm Christ-mas-ing with you.

Hol-i-days are joy-ful, there's al-ways some-thing new. But

Mistletoe and Holly

Words and Music by Frank Sinatra, Dok Stanford and Henry W. Sanicola

First note

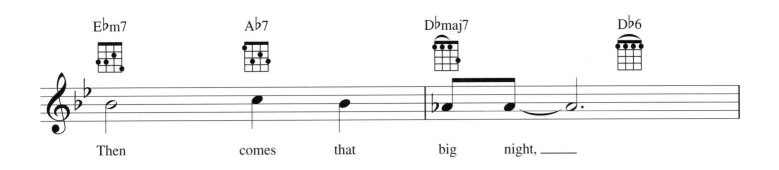

Then comes that big night, _____

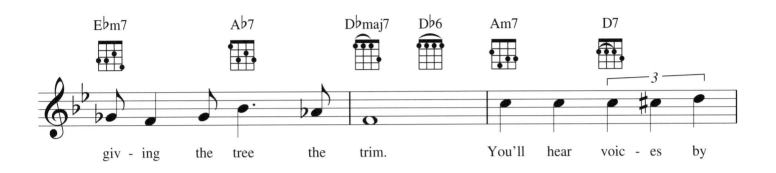

giv-ing the tree the trim. You'll hear voic-es by

D.C. al Coda

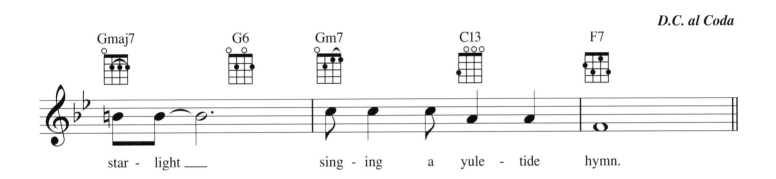

star - light _____ sing - ing a yule - tide hymn.

⊕ Coda

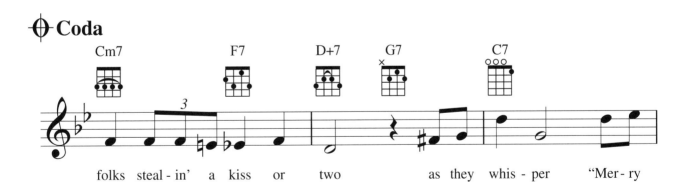

folks steal-in' a kiss or two as they whis-per "Mer-ry

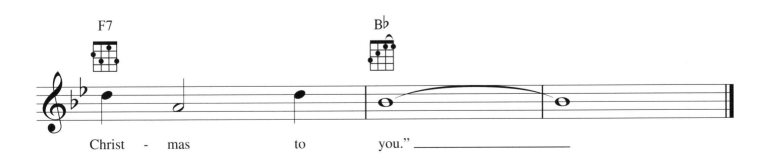

Christ - mas to you." _____

My Favorite Things

from THE SOUND OF MUSIC

Lyrics by Oscar Hammerstein II
Music by Richard Rodgers

blue sat - in sash - es,   snow-flakes that stay on my nose and eye -

lash - es.   Sil - ver white win - ters that melt in - to springs,

these are a few of my fav - or - ite things.   When the

dog bites, when the bee stings,   when I'm feel - ing

sad, _____   I sim - ply re - mem - ber my

fa - vor - ite things and then I don't feel

so   bad.

Rockin' Around the Christmas Tree

Music and Lyrics by Johnny Marks

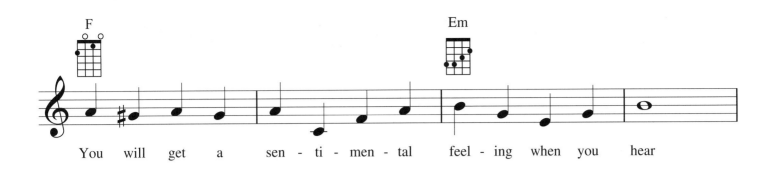

You will get a sen - ti - men - tal feel - ing when you hear

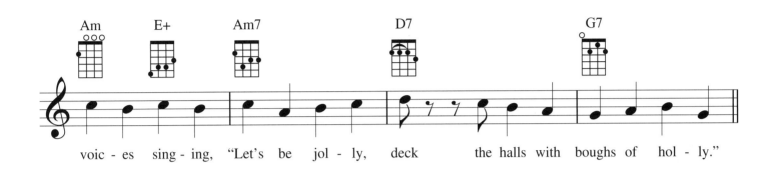

voic - es sing - ing, "Let's be jol - ly, deck the halls with boughs of hol - ly."

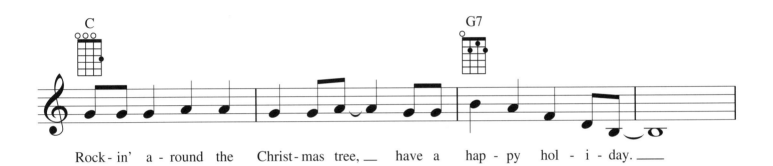

Rock - in' a - round the Christ - mas tree, __ have a hap - py hol - i - day. ___

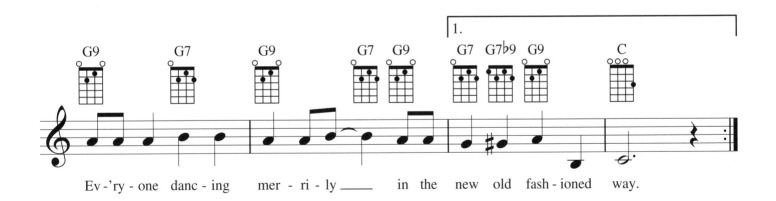

1.

Ev - 'ry - one danc - ing mer - ri - ly ____ in the new old fash - ioned way.

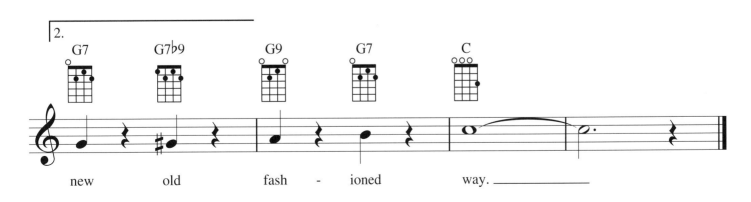

2.

new old fash - ioned way. _____

Rudolph the Red-Nosed Reindeer

Music and Lyrics by Johnny Marks

First note

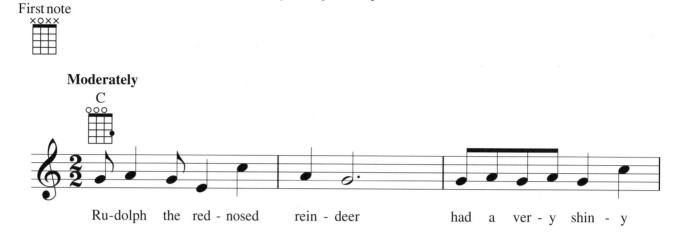

Moderately

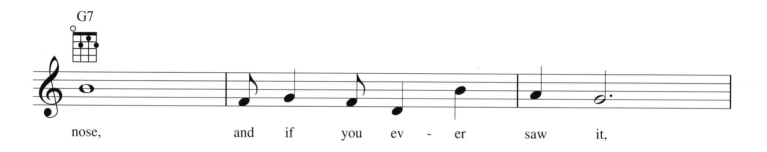

Ru-dolph the red - nosed rein - deer had a ver-y shin-y

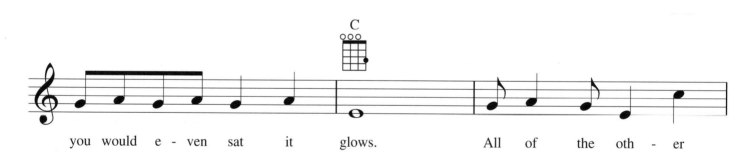

nose, and if you ev - er saw it,

you would e - ven sat it glows. All of the oth - er

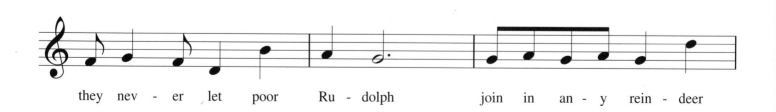

rein - deer used to laugh and call him names;

they nev - er let poor Ru - dolph join in an - y rein - deer

Santa Claus Is Comin' to Town

Words by Haven Gillespie
Music by J. Fred Coots

You bet - ter watch out, you bet - ter not cry.

Bet - ter not pout, I'm tell - ing you why: San - ta Claus is

com - in' to town. He's

mak - ing a list and check - ing it twice, gon - na find out who's

naught-y and nice. San - ta Claus is com - in' to town.

He sees you when you're sleep - in', he knows when you're a -

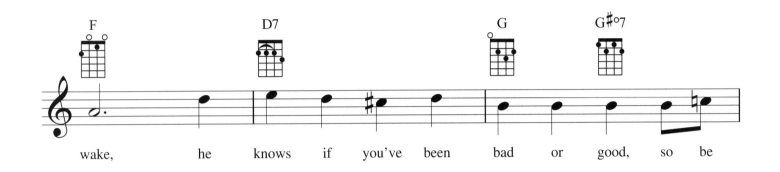

wake, he knows if you've been bad or good, so be

good for good - ness sake. Oh! You bet - ter watch out, you

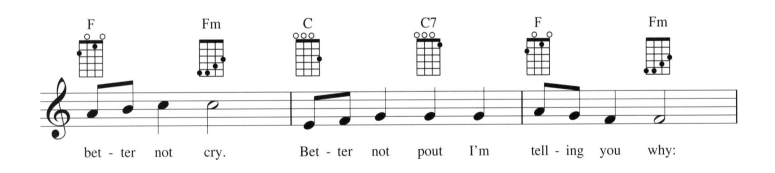

bet - ter not cry. Bet - ter not pout I'm tell - ing you why:

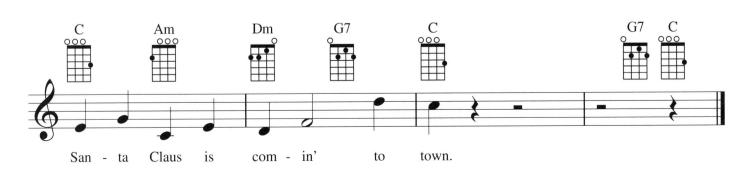

San - ta Claus is com - in' to town.

Silver Bells

from the Paramount Picture THE LEMON DROP KID

Words and Music by Jay Livingston and Ray Evans

Learn To Play Today
with folk music instruction from

Hal Leonard Banjo Method

Authored by Mac Robertson, Robbie Clement & Will Schmid. This innovative method teaches 5-string, bluegrass style. The method consists of two instruction books and two cross-referenced supplement books that offer the beginner a carefully-paced and interest-keeping approach to the bluegrass style.

Method Book 1
00699500 Book $6.95
00695101 Book/CD Pack $16.95

Method Book 2
00699502 ....$6.95

Supplementary Songbooks
00699515 Easy Banjo Solos $6.95
00699516 More Easy Banjo Solos $6.95

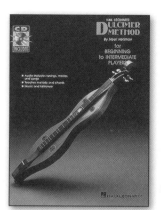

Hal Leonard Dulcimer Method
by Neal Hellman

A beginning method for the Appalachian dulcimer with a unique new approach to solo melody and chord playing. Includes tuning, modes and many beautiful folk songs all demonstrated on the audio accompaniment. Music and tablature.
00699289 Book $6.95
00697230 Book/CD Pack $14.95

Teach Yourself To Play The Folk Harp
by Sylvia Woods

This is the first book written exclusively for the folk harp that teaches the student how to play the instrument, step by step. Each of the 12 lessons includes instructions, exercises and folk and classical pieces using the new skills and techniques taught in the lesson. This is an excellent book for any student, regardless of previous musical training.
00722251 Book $12.95
00722252 Cassette $7.95
00722253 Video $54.95

The Hal Leonard Mandolin Method

Noted mandolinist and teacher Rich Del Grosso has authored this excellent mandolin method that features great playable tunes in several styles (bluegrass, country, folk, blues) in standard music notation and tablature. The audio features play-along duets.
00699296 Book $6.95
00695102 Book/CD Pack $14.95

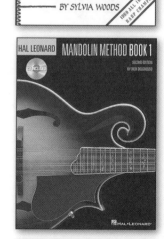

Jumpin' Jim's Ukulele Tips 'N' Tunes
A Beginner's Method and Songbook

This fantastic book for ukulele includes: Amazing Grace • Aura Lee • Bill Bailey, Won't You Please Come Home • (Oh, My Darling) Clementine • Give My Regards to Broadway • He's Got the Whole World in His Hands • Home on the Range • I've Been Working on the Railroad • Let Me Call You Sweetheart • My Country, 'Tis of Thee (America) • Oh! Susanna • She'll Be Comin' 'Round the Mountain • The Star Spangled Banner • Swing Low, Sweet Chariot • When the Saints Go Marching In • You're a Grand Old Flag • and more.
00699406 Ukulele Technique $14.95

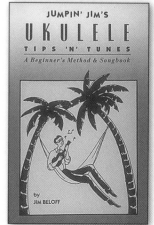

FOR MORE INFORMATION, SEE YOUR LOCAL MUSIC DEALER,
OR WRITE TO:

HAL•LEONARD®
CORPORATION
7777 W. BLUEMOUND RD. P.O. BOX 13819 MILWAUKEE, WI 53213

Visit Hal Leonard Online at
www.halleonard.com

0505

Prices and availability subject to change without notice.

Great Mandolin Publications

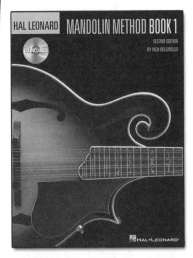
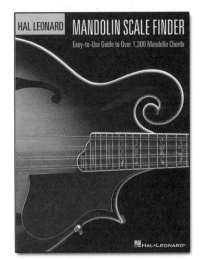
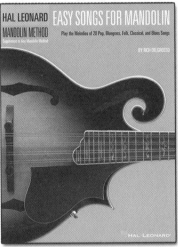
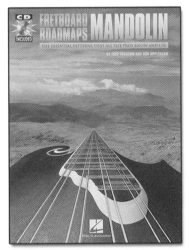
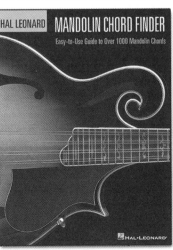

GUITAR SONGBOOKS FOR THE HOLIDAYS

 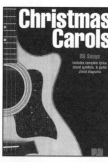 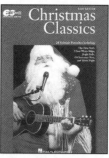   

   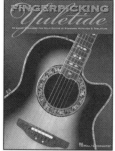  

THE BIG CHRISTMAS COLLECTION FOR EASY GUITAR
Includes over 70 Christmas favorites, such as: Ave Maria • Blue Christmas • Deck the Hall • Feliz Navidad • Frosty the Snow Man • Happy Holiday • A Holly Jolly Christmas • Joy to the World • O Holy Night • Silver and Gold • Suzy Snowflake • You're All I Want for Christmas • and more.
00698978 Easy Guitar with Notes and Tab $16.95 **TAB**

CHRISTMAS CAROLS — GUITAR CHORD SONGBOOK
Includes complete lyrics, chord symbols, and guitar chord diagrams. Includes 80 songs: Angels We Have Heard on High • Away in a Manger • Deck the Hall • Good King Wenceslas • The Holly and the Ivy • Jingle Bells • Joy to the World • O Holy Night • Up on the Housetop • We Wish You a Merry Christmas • What Child Is This? • and more.
00699536 Guitar Chords/Lyrics $12.95

CHRISTMAS CLASSICS
Over 25 easy guitar arrangements of Christmas favorites: Auld Lang Syne • Away in a Manger • Deck the Hall • The First Noel • I Saw Three Ships • Jingle Bells • O Christmas Tree • Once in a Royal David's City • Silent Night • Up on the Housetop • What Child Is This? • and more. Easy guitar arrangements in standard notation and tablature.
00702028 Easy Guitar with Notes and Tab $7.95 **TAB**

CHRISTMAS FAVORITES
A collection of 33 seasonal songs in standard notation and tab. Includes: Angels We Have Heard on High • The First Noel • I Saw Three Ships • Joy to the World • O Come All Ye Faithful • O Holy Night • What Child Is This • and more.
00699097 Easy Guitar with Notes and Tab $9.95 **TAB**

CHRISTMAS SONGS FOR GUITAR
This collection of over 45 favorites showcases songs in their original keys complete with chords, strum patterns, melody and lyrics. Includes: The Christmas Song (Chestnuts Roasting on an Open Fire) • Feliz Navidad • Grandma Got Run over by a Reindeer • I'll Be Home for Christmas • It's Beginning to Look like Christmas • The Most Wonderful Time of the Year • Rockin' Around the Christmas Tree • Silver Bells • and more.
00699247 Strum It Guitar $9.95

CHRISTMAS TIDINGS
23 easy arrangements of Christmas favorites, including: Blue Christmas • The Chipmunk Song • Feliz Navidad • Grandma Got Run Over by a Reindeer • Happy Holiday • I'll Be Home for Christmas • Rudolph the Red-Nosed Reindeer • Silver Bells • and more.
00699123 Easy Guitar with Notes and Tab $9.95 **TAB**

CLASSICAL GUITAR CHRISTMAS COLLECTION
Includes classical guitar arrangements in standard notation and tablature for more than two dozen beloved carols: Angels We Have Heard on High • Ave Maria • Away in a Manger • Canon in D • The First Noel • God Rest Ye Merry, Gentlemen • Hark! the Herald Angels Sing • I Saw Three Ships • Jesu, Joy of Man's Desiring • Joy to the World • O Christmas Tree • O Holy Night • Silent Night • What Child Is This? • and more.
00699493 Guitar Solo $9.95 **TAB**

CONTEMPORARY CHRISTIAN CHRISTMAS
19 contemporary favorites recorded by top artists: Breath of Heaven (Mary's song) • Celebrate the Child • Child of Bethlehem • Emmanuel • Good News • Jesus is Born • One Small Child • Precious Promise • A Strange Way to Save the World • This Gift • This Little Child • and more.
00702170 Easy Guitar with Notes and Tab $9.95 **TAB**

FINGERPICKING CHRISTMAS
20 classics carols: Away in a Manger • Deck the Hall • The First Noel • Go, Tell It on the Mountain • God Rest Ye, Merry Gentlemen • Good King Wenceslas • Hark! The Herald Angels Sing • It Came Upon the Midnight Clear • Jingle Bells • Joy to the World • O Little Town of Bethlehem • Silent Night • We Wish You a Merry Christmas • What Child Is This • and more.
00699599 Solo Guitar $7.95 **TAB**

FINGERPICKING YULETIDE
16 holiday favorites: Blue Christmas • The Christmas Song (Chestnuts Roasting on an Open Fire) • Do You Hear What I Hear? • Frosty the Snow Man • Happy Xmas (War Is Over) • A Holly Jolly Christmas • I'll Be Home for Christmas • Jingle-Bell Rock • Let It Snow! Let It Snow! Let It Snow! • Merry Christmas, Darling • Rudolph the Red-Nosed Reindeer • Silver Bells • This Christmas • and more.
00699654 Solo Guitar $7.95 **TAB**

A FINGERSTYLE GUITAR CHRISTMAS
Over 20 songs for fingerstyle guitar: Auld Lang Syne • Ave Maria • Away in a Manger • The Coventry Carol • Dec.k the Hall • The First Noel • Good King Wenceslas • I Saw Three Ships • Joy to the World • Silent Night • Up on the Housetop • What Child Is This? • and more.
00699038 Fingerstyle Guitar $12.95 **TAB**

THE GUITAR STRUMMER'S CHRISTMAS SONGBOOK
A great collection of 80 favorite Christmas tunes that can be played with open chords, barre chords or other moveable chord types – all in their original keys, complete with chords, strum patterns, melody and lyrics. Includes: The Christmas Song (Chestnuts Roasting on an Open Fire) • Christmas Time Is Here • Do They Know It's Christmas? • Feliz Navidad • Frosty the Snow Man • Grandma Got Run over by a Reindeer • A Holly Jolly Christmas • I Heard the Bells on Christmas Day • I've Got My Love to Keep Me Warm • It's Christmas in New York • Let It Snow! Let It Snow! Let It Snow! • My Favorite Things • O Holy Night • Rudolph the Red-Nosed Reindeer • Silver Bells • We Wish You a Merry Christmas • You Make It Feel like Christmas • and more.
00699527 Melody/Lyrics/Chords $14.95

Prices, contents, and availability subject to change without notice.

FOR MORE INFORMATION, SEE YOUR LOCAL MUSIC DEALER, OR WRITE TO:

HAL•LEONARD®
C O R P O R A T I O N

7777 W. BLUEMOUND RD. P.O. BOX 13819 MILWAUKEE, WI 53213

Visit Hal Leonard online at **www.halleonard.com**